LISTEN:

HOW TO MAKE THE MOST OF YOUR SHORT-TERM MISSION TRIP

A Field Guide for Short-Term Teams

LISTEN:

HOW TO MAKE THE MOST OF YOUR SHORT-TERM MISSION TRIP

Larry McCrary, Melissa Fu, Caleb Crider,
Debbie Stephens, Nathan Sloan

A Field Guide for Short-Term Teams

ISBN: 978-1-7343705-6-0

Unless otherwise indicated, all Scripture quotations are from the Holy Bible, English Standard Version® (ESV®), copyright © 2001 by Crossway, a publishing ministry of Good News Publishers. Used by permission. All rights reserved.

Some of the author's material was used previously in the "Short-Term Ministry Hub Facilitator Training" with TEAM.

For a deeper dive into these topics, check out The Upstream Collective's *Tradecraft: For the Church on Mission*. If your team is interested in further exercises and training pertaining to worldview and your short-term mission trip, please contact The Upstream Collective.

Editor: Meredith Cook
Associate editor: Brad Bell
Cover and interior design: Hayley Moss, Moss Photo and Design

TABLE OF CONTENTS

Part Three: Listen As You Go Back

Appendices

Endnotes

INTRODUCTION
AND PURPOSE

The concept of a mission trip may bring to mind different things, depending on your experience, age, and context. Maybe you think of:

- setting up a medical clinic in a remote mountain village,
- organizing sports camps for children,
- a stomach bug that takes down half of the trip participants,
- spending time building relationships in a foreign context,
- repairing houses as part of disaster relief,
- street evangelism, or
- wearing matching t-shirts and spending far too many hours on a plane together.

No matter what initial image comes to mind, Christ-followers should be no strangers to short-term missions. Yes, mission trips have been promoted within Western church programming for decades, but this particular expression of missions does have its roots in Scripture.

In the Gospel of Luke, we see two prominent examples of "mission trips:"

> *And he called the twelve together and gave them power and authority over all demons and to cure diseases, and he sent them out to proclaim the kingdom of God and to heal... And they departed and went through the villages, preaching the gospel and healing everywhere." (Luke 9:1-2, 6)*

> *After this the Lord appointed seventy-two others and sent them on ahead of him, two by two, into every town and place where he himself was about to go. And he said to them, "The harvest is plentiful, but the laborers are few. Therefore pray earnestly to the Lord*

of the harvest to send out laborers into his harvest. Go your way; behold, I am sending you out as lambs in the midst of wolves." *...The seventy-two returned with joy, saying, "Lord, even the demons are subject to us in your name!" (Luke 10:1-3, 17)*

Later, of course, Jesus commissioned all His followers to "go" as described in His Great Commission. People like Philip, Peter, Paul, Barnabas, and others obeyed that calling in multiple ways. The commission they received and we still receive surely includes the short-term mission trips we know today.

If you're reading this, we're assuming you're going on a short-term mission trip somewhere—whether that's across town or across the globe. So how will you be going?

We're not asking about how you'll get there, who you know on the ground, or if you're partnering with any kind of missions organization. We want you to consider how you will be going in terms of the attitude and posture you'll adopt as you go—as servants, desiring to obey God, etc. But could there be more to **how we go?**

We'd like to suggest that **Christ-followers' approach to mission trips should be primarily based on listening.** That's quite a shift for those of us who are action-oriented and perhaps gifted in administration and organizing these types of opportunities. But could we put our "achiever" mode on hold in order to adopt and prioritize a listening posture?

In this short-term trip field guide, our hope is to help you consider why **listening** truly is the way to make the most of a future short-term trip. We will encourage you to focus your listening on what the Holy Spirit has to say to you about this trip and what He desires for it. We will also help you learn to listen to your teammates, your church leadership, your on-the-ground ministry partners, and to the people and culture of the place you are going.

Now don't get us wrong; we aren't suggesting that your team's preparation solely consists of sitting around in silence (although more of that in our lives is not a bad thing). We'll propose ways you can engage in listening throughout the three parts of your trip: preparation (Before You Go), being on the ground in your destination (As You Go), and after you return home (As You Go Back).

While listening may seem like a simple concept, for those of us who are task-driven, it may be more challenging than one would expect. But the effects can be life-changing for all involved. Ready to get started? Let's make the most of your mission trip.

PART ONE:
LISTEN BEFORE YOU GO

IDENTIFY WHO'S WHO

Preparing to go on your short-term mission trip includes knowing who the key players are in this experience. We'll go over common roles here, but you can personalize this list. Your list will later serve you as you pray.

The Holy Spirit and His Role

Jesus spoke about the most important companion we have in life—and on your upcoming trip:

> *And when he comes, he will convict the world concerning sin and righteousness and judgment... When the Spirit of truth comes, he will guide you into all the truth, for he will not speak on his own authority, but whatever he hears he will speak, and he will declare to you the things that are to come. He will glorify me, for he will take what is mine and declare it to you. (John 16:8, 13-14)*

The Holy Spirit spoke to Philip in Acts 8, sending him to the Ethiopian eunuch:

> *Now an angel of the Lord said to Philip, "Rise and go toward the south to the road that goes down from Jerusalem to Gaza." This is a desert place. (Acts 8:26)*

We see another example when He spoke to Paul through a vision:

> *And a vision appeared to Paul in the night: a man of Macedonia was standing there, urging him and saying, "Come over to Macedonia and help us." And when Paul had seen the vision, immediately we sought to go on into Macedonia, concluding that God*

had called us to preach the gospel to them. (Acts 16:9-10)
Just as Philip and Paul were attentive and listening when the Holy Spirit spoke, our first priority is to listen for what the Holy Spirit wants to say to us. (We'll discuss more of the "how" later.)

How has the Holy Spirit led you to participate in this short-term mission trip? Was it through the encouragement of friends, natural interest, certain Bible verses, or something else? **Write a little about your experience with Him here.**

Your Co-laborers in Christ

Your mission trip is not a solo effort: God is bringing together the people He wants to join Him in specific places, times, and tasks. The Holy Spirit will be working in all of your lives, so it will be important for you to listen to each other.

In addition to your teammates, you probably have at least one team leader from your home church/sending church and at least one on-the-ground "field leader" who serves as the main local point of contact for the trip. If you don't know names yet, find out who they are. (Remember: if you are traveling to a closed country, get used to referring to your local contacts by the name/initial they indicate.)

List your trip leadership and teammates, as well as the names of anyone else you know you'll be partnering with in your destination (local missionaries, marketplace workers, students, local churches, etc.). For further consideration, read Acts 10:1-8: Cornelius' call for Peter.

Supporters from Home

Who has contributed to the trip through prayers, time, resources, or other efforts? List them. What might God want to say to you through their prayers, encouragement, and correspondence? For further consideration, read Acts 13:1-3: The Antioch church commissions Barnabas and Saul.

Those You'll Meet

Some of the most important people to whom you should listen are those whom you haven't even met yet. However, you may have an idea of the profiles of people whom you may meet—and you should leave margin for those God will place in your path unexpectedly. These individuals living in the place(s) you will be visiting can provide great insights into the local culture and worldview—sometimes even what people think about God.

PREPARE IN PRAYER

Listening is a key component of communication in any context; prayer is no exception. Make time to listen for God's priorities in your prayers about this trip, even keeping a prayer journal to record how He moves.

Ask God the following questions, listening for His answer:

1. ***For whom should I be praying?*** *List them again here as God brings them to mind.*

Tip: Remember who is on your "who's who" lists.

2. ***With whom should I be praying?*** *Write down the names of those with whom you will be praying.*

Tip: Are there specific people from your sending church who want to be involved in your trip through prayer? Will you have prayer partners within your team? Will you be praying with your local contacts through video conferences?

3. *How often should I be praying with others?* Write down any prayer rhythms or commitments you make with others to pray together.

Tip: Setting up regular prayer with others can be helpful. In the time leading up to your trip, will there be different prayer emphases in your preparation meetings? Could specific requests be grouped thematically for each team member to pray about during their personal study time on different days? Could you meet with a prayer partner regularly or agree to pray at the same time and day each week about certain requests?

4. *For what should I pray?* List specific topics about which you believe God would have you pray.

Tip: Listening remains key here, as God will reveal different needs via personal study times, logistical preparation, research on where you are going, in virtual meetings with local contacts, and more. Be attentive to the things for which God would have you intercede.

BE A LEARNER

Churches and individuals may unconsciously assume "short-term missions" means going somewhere to teach, show, model, and develop the people they are trying to help. And many trips *are* often related to teaching, working in health care, business leadership training, and more.

However, defaulting to such approaches can make teams come across as know-it-alls, however inadvertently, precisely to those they desire to serve. What if your team deliberately chose to adopt the position of being *learners* instead of experts (even if you are an expert in the task at hand within your context)? After all, prioritizing listening during this experience means you are willing to learn.

Several years ago, a U.S. church asked about coming to Madrid to put on a soccer camp for teenagers. As you can imagine, while the church's intention was good, Spanish kids have grown up playing soccer all their lives, and the very talented ones can even access the Real Madrid or Atlético de Madrid farm teams for youth. So a group of Americans trying to teach local teenagers about the national sport of Spain would have been poorly interpreted.

Instead, a church with the desire to connect with locals over soccer could adopt the position of a learner and sign up to participate in an existing soccer camp. This way, team participants could learn alongside and from the people to whom they wanted to minister, building meaningful relationships on a student-to-student level.

The key is to come into a place and get to know people and be able to share the gospel in a relevant and relational way.

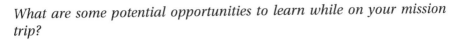

What are some potential opportunities to learn while on your mission trip?

Can you think of situations in which you might find yourself needing to take a backseat and let the locals lead, given their expertise in a certain area, cultural aspect, etc? (Even if your team is conducting something like a medical clinic, what simple things could you learn? Appropriate gestures toward those you will meet? A style of "bedside manner?" A few key phrases in the local language? A children's song from the culture?)

Be creative and expect to hear from the Lord about ways you can be a learner during your trip.

PREPARE FOR BATTLE: SPIRITUAL WARFARE

Your team is seeking God's will, listening to the Holy Spirit, and prayerfully figuring out how to engage meaningfully with those you'll meet during your trip. The team is energized about God's purposes and eager to learn about the host culture and spiritual climate.

In the midst of all this Spirit-led focus and optimism, your team *will* encounter spiritual warfare. It may be blatant or insidious, but it should not be a surprise.

How do you deal with spiritual warfare as a participant in this trip and as a team? How can you tackle such an abstract concept in "power and love and self-control," without fearing the enemy's schemes? (2 Timothy 1:7)

Who is Our Enemy?

The true enemy is not flesh and blood, so no matter how cruel or insensitive someone may be to you, he or she is not actually your enemy. Satan is your accuser, the sower of discord, the discourager—and if you aren't careful, you can react poorly to someone's careless words, a difficult situation, or selfish behavior. These kinds of things can get anyone off track and distracted from what God wants to do.

Read 1 Peter 5:8 and Ephesians 6:12 with your team. *How have you experienced these concepts to be true in your lives? So far in your trip preparation?*

What is True?

Jesus Himself prayed for His followers to know truth. This truth is what believers cling to in times of struggle or despair. Internalizing truth from Scripture has a powerful effect on Christ-followers' attitudes, thoughts, words, and actions during different situations.

Read John 17:15-17 with your team. Echo Jesus' prayer for protection.

What Can I Do with Spiritual Warfare?

Our natural tendencies are to dwell on circumstances rather than the fact that God knew these circumstances before they happened. Taking "every thought captive" (2 Corinthians 10:5), therefore, requires intention. Trust Him; ask Him to help you "capture" your troubling thoughts and replace them with His truth. Then watch Him work through the trying times.

Read 2 Corinthians 10:5 with your team. *List any "arguments and lofty opinions raised against the knowledge of God" that you or your team are facing.*

What Resources Do I Have?

The Lord gives direction on how His followers can protect themselves: by using the "armor" supplied through His Holy Spirit, as well as the defensive weapon of His Word.

Read Ephesians 6:10-18 aloud with your team, pausing to focus on and pray about each piece of armor cited and on the "sword of the Spirit." *List the items here and what quality/characteristic is associated with each.*

Who Will Talk and Pray with Me About This?

Some ways to process and battle spiritual warfare are debriefing together as a team each evening, prayer, and journaling. Verbalizing and praying about struggles shines light into what can seem very dark and troubling.

Read Romans 8:37 with your team. Pray that you will remember that Christ has indeed made you "more than conquerors" in Him.

MAKE A PLAN
TO STAY IN TOUCH

Have you ever considered that you are not the only one invested in your participation in a short-term mission trip? That's right. Others have an interest in the fact that you are joining God in this particular part of His work—and they want to hear from you about it.

Who are these people, and how can you prepare to stay in touch with them?

First, list the following individuals here:

Friends and Family
What loved ones are encouraging and supporting your participation in what God is doing?

Your Sending Church Family and Leadership
Who from your church is sending you and your team on this trip?

Other Supporters
Is your trip being supported financially, logistically, or otherwise by other individuals?

Now consider **what** you'll be sharing with them during this time. Of course, listening comes into play, as you should pay attention to what questions they are asking you (and what they're not asking!). What you tell them about what God is doing can encourage and inspire them as well.

Think about their interest in
- Prayer requests
- People
- Places
- What you'll be doing
- What lessons God seems to be teaching
- Cultural experiences
- Stories
- Other topics they may ask about

Pray with your team about what God will want you to share with those who are interested.

Finally, think about **how** you will stay in touch. Be creative and sensitive to the medium that these individuals use most. Speak with your team-mates and trip leaders to verify that none of these media would jeopardize the security or privacy of the trip or those involved. (When in doubt, ask permission.)

Many teams use these common channels of communication:

- E-mail updates
- Messaging apps
- A password-protected blog/website
- Social media (with discretion and security in mind)
- Meeting in person
- Video conference

What other channels can you think of to stay in touch with those who care about this experience?

DO A LITTLE LANGUAGE LEARNING

If your short-term mission trip will take your team to a place where English isn't the primary language, you may feel intimidated. However, not speaking the local language doesn't have to be a deal-breaker. In fact, in most places, even the most feeble attempt to show interest in the basics of the local language is welcome—and may open some surprising doors.

Not sure where to begin? First, listen to what your team leader and local contacts might have to say. They will likely have recommendations for how to go about learning a few key phrases to help you in your interactions with locals. They may also have ideas for other resources as you prepare.

Start with the basics you would want to know if you were learning English:

- Hello.
- My name is _____. What's yours?
- Please/thank you.
- I don't speak your language well.
- I'm sorry/excuse me.
- Can you please repeat that?
- Goodbye.
- I need help.
- Call the ambulance/police.
- Where is the restroom/bathroom?
- How much does this cost?
- Numbers 1-100
- Do you speak English?

Again, taking the attitude of a listener, a student, and a learner is key.

If you're looking for how to learn these basics and more, here are a few ideas to research:

- Apps from Duolingo, Rosetta Stone, Babbel, and more
- Podcasts: anything from news to actual language-learning shows
- Groups in your hometown who meet up to speak the target language
- Existing social groups/clubs made up of people from your host city or country
- Online language exchange communities (use caution when sharing personal information and certainly, information about the trip)
- Local academies, universities, community colleges, or other organizations that may offer language courses

This list is by no means exhaustive. Explore multiple ideas with your team and your local contacts. Once you're on the ground—don't be afraid! Try out even the little you know, and see what happens. You'll likely learn more than you even expect.

GET READY TO RECEIVE HOSPITALITY

Notions of "hospitality" are usually tied to personal experiences, such as inviting others into your home or organizing a special event focused on someone else. So, what could hospitality have to do with a short-term mission trip if *you* are the guest in the new context?

Actually, hospitality isn't limited to *giving* something to others in a home setting. Sometimes, it has more to do with *receiving* hospitality. Much like taking on the attitude of a learner during the trip, receiving hospitality can be a key part of your role.

Being the recipient of generosity and kindness can be hard for some, but Jesus Himself received hospitality. We regularly find Him willing to be blessed and cared for by others (among them, some unlikely characters, too).

Read the following and jot down from whom Jesus received hospitality, what the expression of hospitality looked like, and in what context the event took place.

Luke 5:29

Luke 7:37-38

Luke 19:5b-6

In Luke 10, Jesus even gave instructions about receiving hospitality to the seventy-two disciples He sent out. For example, verse 8 says, "Whenever you enter a town and they receive you, eat what is set before you."

With this in mind, how can you receive hospitality while on a mission trip? How can you enter another culture with a receptive attitude? This might be a challenge if you only have a "do-for-others" focus. While your intent is to serve and make an eternal impact, no one is a superhero nor savior. You and your teammates are simply followers of Jesus who want to make Him known, but who can also learn and receive from your hosts.

How might you view people differently if you are open to being served by *them*? This is a role-reversal that redirects the heart and mind toward humble acceptance of what others offer that you might just need. You can be a gracious guest in someone else's community, culture, social circles, and home.

This approach allows *both* sides to share the beauty of giving and receiving. You esteem those you encounter as you approach them with an open heart. The Spirit can make this evident through speech and non-verbal communication: an unassuming smile, kind eyes, or a relaxed posture.

Philippians 2:3-5 says, "Do nothing out of selfish ambition or conceit, but in humility consider others as more important than yourselves. Everyone should look not to his own interests, but rather to the interests of others. Adopt the same attitude as that of Christ Jesus..." (CSB)

Following the Great Commission and being faithful to His sending doesn't mean you do all the giving. Receiving hospitality can actually be one of the very ways the gospel can be shared.

List some of the situations and settings in your host city in which you might have the opportunity to receive hospitality (continue on the next page if necessary).

Ask your field leaders and local contacts what hospitality means in the local culture. List their advice regarding receiving hospitality and in what settings hospitality is shown.

TALK ABOUT
MISSIONAL TENSIONS

Ah, tension: an uncomfortable but necessary reality in life. Tensions occur in missions, too, and you and your team may experience some of these tensions as you prepare for and participate in your short-term trip.

Careful: not all tensions are meant to be resolved. Sometimes, they must simply be explored, balanced, held carefully, and certainly, turned over to God.

You might want to talk about the following tensions as a team activity and discuss how they might play out where you are going and in the things you're doing. Take notes below:

PRESENCE vs. PROCLAMATION: *The classic struggle between "being" and "doing;" is mission a task or a natural overflow of identity in Christ? Is the team going to do something (meet physical needs, preach, evangelize, etc.) or to be something (friends, examples, believers in context)? Is it both/and? How?*

MISSIONAL vs. MISSIONARY: *In the West, "missional" usually means an outward-oriented, culturally-aware local ministry. "Missionary," on the other hand, usually implies crossing cultures to communicate the gospel, make disciples, and plant indigenous churches. What is the team's approach?*

RECEPTIVE vs. RESISTANT: *Modern missions has generated a lot of discussion about the prioritization of "unreached" peoples, but what about "reached" places where people are extremely receptive to the gospel? Even on this trip, should the team put its efforts into resistant communities, or should the team "shake the dust from (its) feet," as referenced in Luke 10?*

CREATE vs. JOIN: *Missions engagement begins by meeting people and building relationships with them. Does that mean to start a new club or activity for a certain group of people, or is it better to join existing groups like art classes, neighborhood associations, and recreation leagues? What is the strategy of the local Christian workers the team will meet and partner with?*

PRAGMATISM vs. SPIRIT GUIDANCE: *If something draws a crowd that might actually listen to your team, is it good? What if God leads the team to do some things that do not quickly (or even slowly, or ever) produce visible results? Is it true that "what you win them with, you win them to?" Is it "what works" or "what the team feels called to?"*

EXTRACTION vs. IN-PLACE DISCIPLESHIP: *It's more efficient, safe, and manageable to pull people out of their social circles into "Christian" ones in order to disciple them. But is it the best way? By extracting people from their social influences, are Christ-followers breaking the channels through which the gospel might spread indigenously? Can people be discipled in groups?*

RESEARCH YOUR
HOST CULTURE

So, you're heading into a different culture on your short-term mission trip—oh wait, you're just going to the other side of town? I repeat: so, you're heading into a different culture on your short-term mission trip!

Before you go, do a little homework to learn more about where you're going and who lives there. Check the following sources for insights into local culture, and compare/contrast the information you're seeing from each source. And as always, take in information with an attitude of listening for what God wants you to learn.

List the resources you find, and on the following pages, take notes about what you're learning:

1. Local media: newspapers, radio, television
2. Pop culture and art/literature: music, visual arts, theater, books, and more
3. Podcasts
4. Social media
5. Government or public institution websites (if going to a different country, U.S. and international organizations also publish briefs on countries)
6. Individuals you might already know from your trip destination
7. Information on demographics
8. Documentaries
9. Historical records (written history or data-based)
10. Your own search!

Resources I've Found for Cultural Insights into _____:

PART ONE: LISTEN BEFORE YOU GO

1.

2.

3.

4.

5.

6.

7.

8.

9.

10.

My Notes:

Questions I'd Like to Ask:

DIVE INTO WORLDVIEW

In ministry—particularly in a cross-cultural setting—it is imperative to examine the concept of worldview, starting with our own, and then looking to those with whom we will interact.

By definition, worldview is
1. "the overall perspective from which one sees and interprets the world, and
2. a collection of beliefs about life and the universe held by an individual or a group."[1]

Discovering worldview is like peeling back layers of an onion. If worldview is the core of every human being and behavior is what is seen, then we must dig deeper through the layers of beliefs and values of a culture to get to what has shaped people's perspective.[2]

The only way to do this is through asking questions and listening, which can be done throughout your short-term trip, starting with your preparation.

Spend some time reflecting on what has shaped you and your worldview:

Where and when were you born?

What was it like where you grew up?

What was your economic status?

What was your family life like? How many siblings did you have? Where did you fall in the birth order?

Were you raised in church? Did this influence your relationship with Christ, or did you learn about Him another way?

What world events have happened in your lifetime that have shaped your thinking and how you live?

How have mass media and social media changed in your lifetime? How have they influenced the way you live?

List people who have influenced you positively or negatively during your lifetime. What impact did they have on your life and how you view the world?

What are some things you are learning about your worldview that may make you look at another culture in a different way?

Are you a very task-driven person? How might you have to adjust your behavior or worldview in order to connect with someone in another culture where being task-driven may not be valued?

What are some things that you believe people all over the world have in common?

What are some aspects in which you think cultures differ?

As you have been researching the culture of the place you are going, what are some things about the culture that may seem weird (but are just different) to you?

With whom could you check these perceptions of differences and ask about other aspects of the local worldview?

What are your concerns about being faced with what may be a radically different worldview than your own?

List some ideas of what you can do to deal with these concerns.

If we are not prepared or willing to understand the host culture through its worldview, illuminated by the Holy Spirit, we will not be able to communicate the gospel message in a way that will make sense in the context. As both individuals and as a team, pray regularly for understanding and insight into the local worldview, not with the intent to change it or even to adapt your worldview to it, but to better relate to and effectively interact with those you meet.

TRY OUT A MAPPING EXERCISE

Before going on any type of trip, most people get a map of where they're going and do a little geographical research. This trip should be no different, but you and your team have the opportunity to approach this part of preparation with prayer and with a tool called **mapping**.

Start this activity with a time of listening and silent prayer, and then try out this exercise:

First, quickly sketch a map of where you are now, as if it were for someone who is unfamiliar with the area. Include the significant features in the area, and label them. Share your map with a partner or with the larger group as time allows.

Second, read the following explanation of key mapping elements.[3] Once you've read and understood the concepts, prayerfully mark these elements on your maps.

PATHS: familiar routes people follow. "Paths are the channels along which people customarily, occasionally, or potentially move." The paths we take shape and distort our perspective on the city. *Examples: streets, walkways, transit lines, canals, railroads, etc.*

NODES: places where multiple paths intersect. Nodes "are points, the strategic spots in a city into which an observer can enter, and which are intensive foci to and from which he is traveling. They may be primary junctions, places of a break in transportation, a crossing or convergence of paths, moments of shift from one structure to another." A node is a distinct hub of activity.
Examples: marketplaces, plazas, bus stations, metro stops, or intersections.

DISTRICTS: areas with perceived internal sameness. Districts "are medium-to-large sections of the city, conceived of as having two-dimensional extent, which the observer mentally enters 'inside of,' and which are recognizable as having some common identifying character."
Examples: neighborhoods, suburbs, housing additions, projects, etc.

EDGES: dividing lines between districts. They "are the linear elements not used or considered as paths by the observer." The termination of a district is its edge. Physical proximity does not necessarily mean social similarity.
Examples: shores, railroad cuts, edges of development, walls.

LANDMARKS: points of reference. Defined physical objects: building, sign, store, or mountain. Prominent visual features, usually large and highly visible.
Examples: statues, fountains, monuments, religious centers, distinctive buildings, parks.

Third, now that you've mapped out a familiar place, do a little research to map out the community where you will serve. Use Internet resources; ask your local contacts. This preparation work will contribute to your cultural understanding, as you'll have a better idea of how people experience the city or town where you are going.

*Finally, once you're on the ground, explore as much as is appropriate/ feasible, and check your work against reality through the **"Mapping, Re-visited"** entry. Listen for what God might want to reveal to you along the way.*

LEARN TO TELL A FEW STORIES

In the traditional missions mindset, "sharing your testimony" is pivotal; however, listening before launching into telling your story with Jesus is even more important.

One young European believer encapsulated a common viewpoint on this exact issue to a group of primarily American Christians. She explained that she had concluded that the typical American approach to "telling others about Jesus" was word-vomiting one's entire spiritual journey, often using Christian-only language and ignoring cultural context, which she said she found, even as a Christ-follower, both personally overwhelming and culturally invasive.

Sometimes Christians prepare to "share their testimony" in an unintentionally aggressive way, often ignoring the Holy Spirit's prompting to listen, cultural cues, or personal bias of the other person. This subconscious approach can be a result of nerves, fear, or at worst, pride.

This is why listening first is so important when it comes to talking about faith at home or elsewhere. Listening to the Holy Spirit will help you first to understand your relationship with God: how it started and how it has grown and matured. Listening to Him will also help you discern when He wants you to tell someone something about Him, what, and how.

Listening to your local believing contacts will aid you in understanding key cultural concepts, language, nonverbals, and social dynamics when talking about weighty and spiritual matters. Listening to the person you are engaged in conversation with will help you know what is appropriate to share, at what point, and how that person might best understand the message.

None of this is to say you will never hear the Holy Spirit prompt you to share your testimony in the "traditional" sense. You must follow His lead first and foremost. But in many contexts, a smaller storytelling approach is much more sensitive, appropriate, impactful, and even frequent! These smaller testimonies may open the door for more extensive conversations.

Let's get to it!

1. *Sit in silence for a few minutes, listening to God.*

2. *Ask Him what He wants you to reflect on about your story with Him:*
   a. *First, think about your story as a whole. (Thank Him all along the way.)*
   b. *Then, ask Him to bring to mind specific points/experiences with Him that have been significant in your spiritual journey. List your experiences here.*

3. *Pray more about those specific points and experiences. How might they relate to the local culture where you're going? How might people there relate to the stories God is bringing to mind?*

4. *Use the next pages to write out those pivotal experiences and events. Describe the following:*
    a. *Where were you?*

b. *How old were you?*

c. *What was your family and social situation at the time?*

d. *What led up to those key moments, experiences, and processes?*

e.   What was the outcome?

Remember that each spiritual milestone does involve a story, which can be told as such: setting the scene, explaining the conflict, building to a climax, and reflecting on the outcome and resolution.

5. *Practice telling your story(-ies) with teammates and even your local believing contacts, if available. Listen to any questions or feedback they might have (not on the story itself, but on how you tell it).*
6. *Keep praying and listening to God, expecting His discernment in how you share these testimonies.*

PREPARE FOR GOSPEL CONVERSATIONS

Let's take away the pressure, stress, and guilt related to what it means to "share the gospel." Christ-followers can feel these things because they assume they are solely responsible for this task.

That idea couldn't be more wrong.

God is faithful to make His good news known, and He will use you. You only have to listen to Him and follow His lead.

Paul implores the church at Colosse, "pray also for us that God may open to us a door for the word, to speak the mystery of Christ..." (Colossians 4:3, CSB). God Himself opens the door for His message—you don't have to push your way in.

So what place does the gospel have in conversations with others? Every. Single. Place. Don't underestimate God's creativity in inserting Himself into conversations and giving you amazing, unusual opportunities to discuss His love.

How can you listen and discern those moments and enter into gospel conversations?

1. **Prayer.** Even though your short-term mission trip schedule may be wild, time for personal and corporate prayer must take priority.

2. **Know the gospel itself.** You don't have to be a theologian or expert in apologetics to discuss the gospel, but the more you know and internalize the good news of Christ, the more apparent His relevance in every conversation will be. Study the Scripture; pore

over it; ask the hard questions; talk about it among your group.

3. **Check your own motives.** How are you approaching sharing the gospel? Anxiously? From a position of cultural superiority? Assuming people have never heard anything about Jesus? Wanting to have all the answers? (We identify these things because we've been there. These are often hidden motives juxtaposed with true desires to love people and make Christ known.)

4. **Listen to your local Christ-following contacts.** Whether they are originally from the host city/country or not, they are living in the local culture and can give invaluable insights into what role spirituality and religion play, what is appropriate to discuss, important language to use/avoid, etc.

5. **Go back to your cultural research.** You may be surprised to learn even before you go that there are natural bridges to the gospel within a community and culture. What are the current issues? How do people celebrate? What are the questions people are asking? What do people not discuss? Often, these cultural aspects can prove to be conversational open doors.

6. **Listen to those you meet.** In conversation, our values, hopes, priorities, and personalities are revealed. Enter into a conversation desiring to listen and get to know the person(s), regardless of whether a door is opened to ask or speak about Jesus in that moment.

ASK QUESTIONS

In "Be a Learner," you saw how this trip is the perfect opportunity to put yourself into the role of a humble student who can explore the culture of the city/country where your team is going. A great part of being a learner is asking questions and listening prayerfully to the answer given.

For some naturally curious or extraverted people, the desire to pelt a local acquaintance with all kinds of questions may feel irresistible. For others who may feel intimidated by the new context or who aren't naturally given to asking questions, embracing the concept may be more difficult.

So what could asking questions look like on your trip, and how can it benefit all involved?

1. **Ask your cultural insiders about asking questions.** Before you go, it's helpful to know how asking questions can generally be perceived in the context. While sometimes curiosity is appreciated, at other times, it can come across as invasive, threatening, or as an interrogation. Your local guides can help you navigate.

2. **It's beneficial to listen and observe before asking a question.** You may not have to put a lot of thought into questions like, "does the city bus accept a tourist transportation pass?" However, if you're seeking to understand the community where you are going and want to ask deeper questions, a little reflection beforehand is good.

3. **Play the tourist card.** If appropriate, sometimes prefacing a question with, "I'm visiting this place for the first

time, and I wondered if I might ask you about..." can both pave the way for a more open response or disarm someone who might feel defensive about being asked something.

4. **Go deeper than "yes" or "no."** It's true. You may occasionally meet someone from your host culture who doesn't really want to engage in conversation. But you have a chance at decent, interesting dialogue if you ask questions that require more than a one-word answer and potentially allow those you meet to open up.

5. **Be genuine.** Ask questions because you actually want to know, not to try to force a conversation about spiritual things. God will lead you even in your questions so you will both learn and honor the person with whom you're speaking. Enjoy the conversation, and if God wants to open a door for more meaningful topics, He will.

6. **Listen to people's answers.** Questions give you a chance to learn, so don't just fire off questions without paying attention to the answers. Truly listen and engage. It will form a great basis for a relationship even during the short duration of your trip.

List questions you already have about the place you are going and the people you'll meet. As you research and pray, update your list. Pray over which questions you might ask before the trip and which ones you might ask those you meet as you get to know the people and the culture.

THINK THROUGH TEAM DYNAMICS

Apart from listening to the Holy Spirit about what He has in mind for your trip, you should also prepare to listen to what He wants to say to you about you! You and your teammates' relational dynamics while serving together is crucial, so one way to start addressing that dynamic is through self-reflection.

Being a "sent one" requires self-reflection in order to understand yourself better. Personality profiles and assessment tools can help you think about your personality type, strengths and weaknesses, and how you best relate to others. Some are available for free or for a fee online; others may be available in print. (Ask your team leaders about the possibility of the entire team going through an assessment to address interpersonal communication and team dynamics.)

Although there are many different traits and behaviors that can be studied through self-reflection, start by looking at 1) introversion vs. extraversion and 2) approaches to conflict resolution.

Introversion vs. Extraversion[4]

Differences between introverts and extraverts tend to manifest themselves pretty quickly in a group, especially in an experience as intense as a mission trip.

Introverts often
- desire private space and time.
- become drained around large groups of people.
- need time alone to recharge.
- are reserved, quiet and deliberate; they act cautiously when

meeting people.
- form a few deep attachments.
- communicate best one-on-one.

Extraverts often
- are social; they are energized by other people and they wither or fade when alone.
- draw energy from people.
- communicate with excitement and enthusiasm with almost anyone in the vicinity.
- demonstrate high energy and noise.
- share personal information early.

Can you see how these differences may cause a few issues when traveling together? However, look at the positive side to see how God has uniquely provided for gospel proclamation. An extravert can start conversations with anyone and be right in his or her element. In the same setting, an introvert will excel at one-on-one relationship-building. Both can experience gospel intentionality with those they meet.

Understanding the differences between these two simple personality traits can go a long way so that groups can build on each person's strengths and complement each other's weaknesses.

With which of these characteristics do you identify? What do your teammates think? Where do they fall on this particular spectrum?

Conflict Resolution

Even if everyone on your team believes they are self-aware, interpersonal conflict can still arise. If one person's needs or expectations (whether expressed or not) are not met by the other person(s) involved, or if there is a clash of interests, conflict shows up.

Resolving conflict, especially among Christ-followers, is critical to healthy, mature relationships. It is even more important in a short-term mission trip setting for everyone to be unified to work through conflict for the good of those involved and for the whole team.

Prayerfully listen to the Lord and answer the following questions:

How do you personally respond to conflict? (Remember, here, the goal is self-reflection—not writing what you think the answer "should be.")

Do you have a tendency to shut down or perhaps suppress your feelings when faced with conflict?

Do you become aggressive and outspoken if in conflict with someone?

Think of an example of a situation in which you and someone else were able to resolve conflict successfully. How did you do it? Why did you think it was important?

Conflict is difficult, and people deal with it differently. It is perhaps most tempting to deal with conflict by NOT dealing with it—by avoiding or denying it. Others may find themselves drawn to outright aggressive attitudes and words. But if you can look at conflict as an unmet need or expectation, it makes it less personal, and you can avoid these extremes and other hurtful behaviors that negatively affect team dynamics.

When faced with conflict, ask someone objective to help you identify the source of the conflict (again, usually unmet needs or expectations) and talk through the situation with the other party. You will likely discover that the other person also had an unmet need or expectation. You can then all work together to see if those needs/expectations can or should be met.

You can be sure that Satan would love to use something simple to discredit or dismantle the ministry God has sent you to do. So don't avoid the conflict, which is what most people do, or lash out at the other party. Instead, remember that each of you should "look not only to his own interests, but also to the interests of others." (Philippians 2:4)

Finally, keep in mind that "we do not wrestle against flesh and blood, but against the rulers, against the authorities, against the cosmic powers over this present darkness, against the spiritual forces of evil in the heavenly places." (Ephesians 6:12)

Interpersonal conflict on a team is inevitable at some point, but with a group committed to prayerfully and humbly seek resolution, God can use even those situations to unify the team and draw each person closer to Himself.

BE AN EFFECTIVE TEAM MEMBER

We've touched on listening to the Holy Spirit, to your teammates, and to locals and the host culture, but your team should also listen to another set of key players: those who are leading your trip.

Most short-term mission trips involve a team leader from the sending church, as well as individual(s) on the ground where the team is going, sometimes called the "field leader." The field leader may be a local believer who is coordinating the trip on the ground or a cross-cultural worker who lives there. Since he or she is immersed in the culture, he or she will be an invaluable reference for practical and cultural insights. Your team leader will listen and adhere to what the field leader instructs the team to do.

We highlight these individuals because their roles are important—but so is the role of each and every team *member*. Being unified in following the instructions, advice, and example of these leaders is part of being an effective team member on this trip.

Even if you have previous experience with the host culture, it's important to trust the guidance of the team and field leaders. They have been prepared for their roles and can share valuable knowledge based on their past experiences with the contexts and tasks at hand. They are also trained in the larger strategy of which this trip forms a part.

Now, we aren't saying you should follow blindly and never ask questions. However, if you do have questions, keep an open, respectful dialogue about anything you are unsure about. Open, clear, and kind communication among all leaders and team members is key.

These leaders need committed, effective team members during this intense trip. Likewise, you should depend on them to cast a vision for what God is doing, for help understanding aspects of the trip, and certainly, for support in team dynamics.

What are concrete ways you can be an effective team member?

1. **Pray for your team and its leaders.** Both the team leader and the field leader would welcome prayers for their responsibilities and roles. Make sure to pray for them with your teammates/prayer partners within the team.

2. **Listen** to the instructions given regarding safety, protocol, cultural norms, etc., and follow them. Instructions are given for the health, safety, and effectiveness of the team.

3. **Commit** to the unity of your team. Praying for and supporting one another as you get to know each other is critical. But as mentioned in the "Team Dynamics" piece, healthy conflict resolution is also key. As you prepare, agree together on how to handle interpersonal conflict and tension on the trip.

4. **Get to know your leaders.** Neither team nor field leaders are supposed to be generals, barking out orders. Get to know these individuals who have been called to use their gifts in facilitating this experience. This trip is an opportunity to learn from someone new.

5. **Ask** how else you can support the leadership. Could your leaders delegate a certain task to you? Do they need additional accountability? Can you take them anything special from your home country to show your appreciation for their time and effort?

6. *List your other ideas here. How do you think you can be an effective team member?*

STAY HEALTHY

Health is one of your main goals in preparing for a short-term trip. You're on the ground for a short time and you don't want to miss out on opportunities God has planned for you. Keep these tips in mind if your trip has an international destination, and listen to advice from others who have experience in this type of trip:

Before you go:
- Research any local health risks via the country's Consular Information Sheet and the CDC. Does your destination country (or any layover countries) have any travel restrictions, health requirements, etc?
- Avoid others with colds or viruses.
- Get adequate rest, drink lots of water, and exercise. Depending on the context, you may walk much more than you do in your home setting.
- Visit a doctor for any required immunizations for the area. Ask about a broad-based antibiotic to take if needed for skin or parasite infections.
- Obtain overseas travel insurance, including emergency medical evacuation.
- Update medical prescriptions.
- Know where the closest hospitals are located; see which are best for foreigners.
- If needed, bring appropriate facial coverings such as medically graded masks.

Prepare a small medical kit that contains:
- Tweezers
- Digital thermometer

- Anti-diarrheal medication
- Hydrocortisone cream
- Antibiotic cream
- Allergy medication
- Insect repellent
- Water purification tablets
- Epinephrine pen (if needed)
- Oral rehydration salts
- Variety of bandages and sterile dressings
- Antiseptic towelettes

In an international context ...

- Drink plenty of bottled water to stay hydrated. Make sure the seal has not been broken.
- Brush teeth with bottled water.
- Avoid ice in drinks in developing countries.
- Eat only cooked vegetables and fruit that you can peel yourself. Fresh fruit and vegetables look beautiful but can be washed with contaminated water. **Cook it; peel it; boil it; or forget it!**
- Avoid eating at street vendors.
- "Fire is your friend!" Eating places where you can see food is cooked over a hot flame will cut down on bacterial infections from food.
- Wash hands frequently and use hand sanitizer before eating.
- Wear comfortable shoes.
- Be aware of your surroundings.
- Use sunscreen as appropriate.
- Be sure to purchase enough face masks to use while traveling and on site as many countries will require the use of masks in many public places.

IMPORTANT: *Travelers who suffer from chronic or pre-existing conditions should carry their medical history with them at all times.*

Remember: you never want to offend someone who is hosting you in their home by refusing to eat something they are serving. However, you can be wise in what and how much you eat by choosing certain things over others, such as cooked foods. (Don't finish things off too quickly, as your host may want to keep filling your plate.)

PLAN FOR OVERSEAS SAFETY AND SECURITY

The best way to deal with a crisis is to avoid it. Along with staying healthy, minimizing risk and managing potential or real crises is fundamental. Keep in mind these potential risks and tips for how to prepare and deal with them:

Administrative: Loss of passport or important documents. Before you leave, research pertinent embassy locations for where you will be traveling.

Health and Safety: Purchase travel medical insurance that includes emergency medical evacuation. Several companies offer this type of coverage and there are some companies who often work specifically with faith-based trips. Research medical care for where you are going, including the closest hospitals, and carry that contact information.

Natural Disaster: Create a contingency plan.
- Identify a rally point such as a hotel or landmark.
- Identify what key person should receive information in case phone and Internet service are unavailable. Determine how they will receive that information.
- Register with the STEP program in case evacuation is necessary.
- Know the best route to exit the country and how to buy bus, plane, or train tickets.

Food and Water Safety: See "Stay Healthy."

Common Crime Threats:
- Pickpocketing: Secure money and passport in front pockets or under your clothing. Never carry anything you don't want to lose.

If you are a victim, don't fight back; your life is more important!

- Mugging/burglary: Maintain physical and situational awareness to minimize being a soft target.
- Carjacking: Keep car windows and doors locked when traveling by car.
- Identity theft: Be careful what networks and sites you use in public places, as personal or financial information could be compromised.

Less-Common Crime Threats:
- Civil Unrest: avoid public demonstrations and be vigilant in crowds or in other large gatherings.
- Kidnapping
- Sexual Assault: don't venture out alone. Take a teammate or local contact with you.

Information Security:
- Sanitize computers/smartphones before going by taking off potentially sensitive information.
- Encrypt or password protect electronic devices.
- Back up computers before leaving.

On the next few pages, write down the action plan your team is taking on both a group and individual basis, including any specific assignments to team members and advice from locals.

PART ONE: LISTEN BEFORE YOU GO

PART ONE: LISTEN BEFORE YOU GO

PACK SMART; PACK LIGHT

If you're asking what on earth to pack on your short-term mission trip, listen to what some seasoned veterans have to say.[5]

Pack Smart

Do your research in order to pack smart. Keep three things in mind when you pack:

- Climate: find out about average temperature and rainfall for the area where you are going.
- Culture: a team member traveling to France will pack very differently from someone going to India. However, keep in mind the specific culture with which you are working. Even if you're going to France, you may be working with diaspora peoples that are more conservative.
- The nature of your tasks: if you are going to be backpacking in the Himalayas, you're going to need more than a good attitude!

Basic guidelines for packing clothing:

- choose modest styles—based on *that* culture, not what is considered "modest" where you live.
- comfortable, but not sloppy.
- low-maintenance clothes in basic colors. Try to stay away from clothing that is too flashy.
- washable, quick dry fabrics; no dry clean only.
- layer clothes for cold weather rather than taking bulky sweaters.
- no potentially controversial messaging (avoid American flags, political statements, and Christian references unless your team leader tells you it is all right.)

Know your ministry location. Ask questions. Make a list. And remember, less is more!

Pack Light

Pack only what you can carry. Literally. You may be dashing to catch connecting flights, chasing trains pulling away from stations, and hauling your luggage up stairs. You should be able to run without being burdened by your luggage.

Remember, one way to minimize packing is to take a few extremely versatile articles of culturally appropriate clothing and shoes so you can mix-and-match. In many cultures, no one will be shocked if you wear the same piece of clothing more than once during your time. Simplify and pack only what you absolutely need.

Remember your baggage limit:

1. Plan to limit yourself to one checked bag. If your team leader confirms an additional bag is allowed, it can be used to take ministry supplies or host/field leader gifts if needed.
2. Know the baggage weight limit and stick to it. Airlines are increasingly strict about weight and size limits for both checked and carry-on luggage. Consult your team leader or the airline you will be traveling on about limits for each type of bag.

Need some packing suggestions? Check the "Pack Your Bags" entry in the Appendices.

PART TWO:
LISTEN AS YOU GO

LISTEN TO THE SPIRIT AS YOU GO

Forget "unreached people groups," your "strategic focus," or "what works;" the only guide for mission is the Holy Spirit. Jesus concluded His instructions to "make disciples of all nations" with "I am with you always" (Matthew 28:18-20). He did this to establish His authority to send and guide His followers in His mission, no matter the expression or context.

Believers' necessary dependence on the step-by-step leadership of the Holy Spirit is often an afterthought in mission. It's easy to consult Him once, then ask for His blessing on the strategy developed rather than allow Him to guide every turn along the way.

When Paul was on his second mission trip, the Holy Spirit sometimes frustrated his strategy for mission. In Acts 16:6, we read that Paul had been "forbidden by the Holy Spirit to speak the word in Asia," even though that region was full of unreached people who had never heard the gospel.

Then in verse 7, when Paul's team "attempted to go into Bithynia," "the Spirit of Jesus did not allow them." Paul's tactic was to preach where no one else had, but his strategy was to consult the Spirit before doing anything.

If the Spirit were to forbid you from doing something as essential to your mission as preaching the gospel in the way, time, or place you had envisioned, what would you do? If He prevented you from meeting some obvious need, would you recognize it as Him?

Our mission depends on the Holy Spirit's guidance every step of the way.

What are some instances when you have sensed the leadership of the Holy Spirit related to this trip or past trips?

Has He ever done or shown you anything unusual that went against your initial plans? List examples.

How did you react to that new opportunity or redirection? What happened?

Set aside time to pray individually and collectively about this all-important topic.

MAPPING, REVISITED

Remember the mapping exercise we encouraged you to try before you left home? Now's your chance to put those skills into practice on the ground and contrast any draft you might have prepared with the reality around you.

As you explore your new surroundings, keep in mind the concepts we've already highlighted:

PATHS: familiar routes people follow. *Examples: streets, walkways, transit lines, canals, railroads, etc.*

NODES: places where multiple paths intersect. *Examples: marketplaces, plazas, bus stations, metro stops, or intersections.*

DISTRICTS: areas with perceived internal sameness. *Examples: neighborhoods, suburbs, housing additions, projects, etc.*

EDGES: dividing lines between districts. *Examples: shores, railroad cuts, edges of development, walls.*

LANDMARKS: points of reference. *Examples: statues, fountains, monuments, religious centers, distinctive buildings, parks.*

How would you modify the draft you prepared?

What new things have you discovered? What has surprised you?

What questions do you have for your field leaders and local contacts related to your surroundings?

Share your comparisons, contrasts, and map updates among your team. Listen prayerfully for their insights and feedback.

As you continue reading through this "As You Go" section, you may wish to identify other things on your map. As a team, share these new insights during your Daily Debriefing (see the "As You Go Back" section).

OBSERVE

Now that you're on the ground, you have a great chance to continue your role as a learner through observation of your host city and culture. The best way to learn social norms is to observe and mimic them, so why not try it out?

As appropriate for your setting, visit the following places and watch people. Spend thirty minutes in each location. Be sure to take notes in the space provided about what you observe.

Remember: people don't usually appreciate being stared at and may misinterpret your intentions. If someone asks, however, it may be a great opportunity to explain that you are trying to learn more about the city/community/culture and perhaps ask some questions about what you are observing—of course, prayerfully listening for their answers.

OUTDOOR PUBLIC SPACE (Usually free.)

- *How do people greet/leave one another?*
- *How are people dressed? What clues does this give about a person's place in daily life? How do couples interact? Families? Co-workers?*
- *What type of activities happen on the street?*
  What types of buildings/commerce do you see?

PUBLIC TRANSPORTATION (You must be a paying customer.)

- *Who do you see riding the train? The bus?*
- *What seem to be the "rules" for behavior on public transportation?*
  How do people carry their belongings?
- *How does someone seem to select where to sit/stand/ride?*

RESTAURANT OR CAFETERIA (Be sure to buy something!)

- *Who do you see in the restaurant?*
- *What function does the restaurant seem to serve for the people here?*
  What do people order? What do they do with leftovers?
- *How long do people seem to stay?*
  How do people pay? Do they leave tips?

PRAYER WALK

Prayer walking is described as "praying *on*-site with *in*sight."[6] If you're not familiar with this practice, it is a unique, active way to pray while you move around a neighborhood, engaging your senses and your spirit with what God is doing in the area.

Prayer walking is intercession on location, with information, in cooperation, against opposition, for God's glory. Through prayer walking, cultural insight can be gained through observation and interaction. Spiritual insight also comes through prayerfully being present on site.

The mechanics are simple: pray as you walk (or ride the subway, hop on a bus, or drive—eyes open, of course), and observe the environment, listening to what God may be saying. Interact with Him and intercede for the neighborhood as you take note of what you see.

Remember: intercessory prayer is simply speaking to God on behalf of others. Paul described it well: "I urge that supplications, prayers, intercessions, and thanksgivings be made for all people..." (1 Timothy 2:1).

If possible, try out a prayer walk with your team before you leave home. Once you have arrived at your destination, use prayer walking to explore the area (if appropriate) for the culture and city.

Prayer walking offers unique opportunities such as:

- Intimacy with God.
- Intentional intercession.
- Prayer in response to what you see and hear.
- Sensitivity to what God reveals to you through Scripture and the

Holy Spirit.
- Asking at the place of need.
- Seeing through God's eyes.
- Steps of faith and obedience.

Prayer walking doesn't have to take just one form, either. See what is appropriate for the host culture.

This activity can include aspects such as:

- Praying silently.
- Praying out loud.
- Asking forgiveness for personal sins.
- Singing songs.
- Reading and praying Scripture.
- Specific short, conversational prayers.
- Walking slowly around buildings and in public spaces.
- Sitting on benches.
- Standing at overlook points.
- Stopping to reflect and listen or discuss insights.
- Looking for clues as to how to pray for people's needs.
- Being sensitive to divine appointments and connecting with people as the Spirit prompts you.

Here are some suggestions for areas of prayer:

- Government buildings, especially those that may affect ministry.
- Churches or locations for possible new church starts.
- High places (mountains, towers) you see that provide perspective of the area.
- Neighborhoods or areas where there is no known presence of Christ-followers.
- Schools, academies, and universities.
- Hospitals, clinics, and pharmacies.
- Business districts.
- Religious sites and places of spiritual influence.

After your prayer walk in your own community, take a few notes in preparation for a potential opportunity in your destination.

What was your experience like?

What did you notice on your prayer walk?

Where did you sense God working? Did you feel led by the Spirit to move in a certain direction geographically, intercede for specific things, or interact with anyone? How?

How do you think prayer walking can be incorporated where you are going?

Ask your team and field leaders if such an exercise would be feasible. If so, when could your team do it? How should you approach the activity?

LOOK FOR A PERSON OF PEACE

In your host city, God has been preparing "persons of peace" for you and your teammates to meet. Isn't that exciting?

A person of peace is someone God has prepared to receive the gospel into a community of people, according to Luke 10:6. He or she usually has the following characteristics:[7]

A Person of Receptivity: someone sovereignly prepared by God (before your arrival) to receive the gospel. The concept is not "sow, and then harvest," but "harvest (what God has sown) and then sow."

- Pray for the person of peace.
- Search until you find His person of peace.
- If you don't find him or her, pray about where he or she may be. Follow God's lead there.

Examples of the Person of Peace: Zacchaeus (Luke 19), Cornelius (Acts 10), Lydia (Acts 16), the Philippian jailer (Acts 16). (You may wish to read the accounts of these individuals with your teammates.)

A Person of Reputation: He or she has a known reputation, either good or bad. The person could be a politician, a prostitute, a business leader, a warlord, a drug dealer, a community hero, a social influencer, or any number of other figures.

A Person of Referral: News about who Jesus is spreads word-of-mouth. The person of peace actively shares the Good News with others, pointing them back to Jesus. The gospel "goes viral."

FINDING A PERSON OF PEACE

According to Luke 10:2-11, a person of peace will:

- Welcome you.
- Speak kindly to you.
- Be a person of hospitality, inviting you into his or her circles.
- Have a heart of compassion.
- Share a similar vision.
- Sense the need for change.
- Make a way for you into his or her social circles.
- Risk his or her reputation for you.
- His or her approval will endear you to his or her friends.

It may seem hard to believe, but a person of peace will be an instant friend who will open the door to others. It is a unique and creative design God has put into place. Once you discover a person of peace, get to know him or her. Let that person be your friend and cultural guide. As you listen to this person of peace, you will no doubt gain insights on what God is up to in the community.

Pray about and for the persons of peace you will meet, and ask to be attentive to God's leadership to them during your trip.

FIND THE THIRD PLACES

Your team has arrived at your destination, and you're eager to explore and continue listening "as you go." Take a quick dive into urban sociology to help as you engage with your host community, courtesy of Ray Oldenburg, author of The Great Good Place, in reference to a concept called the "third place:"

1. The "first place" in a community is one's home.
2. The "second place" is where one works or goes to school.
3. The "third place" is where a person connects socially and processes information communally.

Third places can be considered "anchors" of community life that facilitate and foster broad, creative interaction. All societies have informal meeting places; in modern times they've become a vital societal need.[8]

What do these third places look like, then?

- Comfortable, relaxing, inviting
- Free or inexpensive food and drink
- Highly accessible
- High proximity for many, usually within walking distance
- Involve regulars
- New and old friends found there

As you might expect, third places might be cafés, tea shops, community centers, parks, beauty parlors, markets, bars, etc.

As your team explores your new surroundings, ask yourselves (and even local contacts) these questions to discover the community's third places:

- Where do people go to share really good news?
- Where do people process information and ask, "what does this mean for us?"
- Where do people go to relax, where they're neither host nor guest, yet both?
- How do people interact within the space?
- What are the rules?
- Who hangs out here?
- Who's allowed? Who's not?

In *Exiles: Living Missionally in a Post-Christian Culture,* missiologist Michael Frost writes, "In today's society, any attempt to model your life on the life of Christ must include a genuine attempt to hang out regularly in third places."[9]

Jesus does set the example of deliberately being present in third places:

- Eating with "sinners" (Matthew 9:10)
- The city gates (John 5:2) and squares (Matthew 11:1)
- In synagogues (Matthew 4:23)
- On hillsides (Matthew 5:1), at shorelines (Matthew 4:18), in gardens (Matthew 26:36)

What public spaces do your local contacts identify as "third places?"

How can your team follow Christ's example during your trip, deliberately putting yourselves in third places? List your ideas.

DISCOVER LOCAL TRIBES

Maybe your team is getting the lay of the land by now—mapping, prayer walking, becoming familiar with your host community surroundings. But what would a community be without people?

To help you better understand and get to know the locals you'll meet on your short-term mission trip, let's explore the concept of *tribes*—and no, it's not limited to mission trips to remote places.

The truth is, people live in tribes. We relate to society by attaching ourselves to certain people. Historically (and in developing nations), tribes are clan/family based. In developed nations, tribes are voluntary and tend to be based on affinity.

Some examples of tribes:

- Maasai of Kenya and Tanzania (closed, family-based)
- High school cliques (closed, identity-based)
- Apple computer users (open, identity-based)
- Instagram influencer followers (open, personality-based)
- The Catholic Church (closed, tradition/participation-based)

No matter the context, tribes are the social circles in which people move. These groups clearly define who is "in" and who is "out." It can be difficult to get involved in people's lives because almost everyone already has some social network: group(s) of friends that have a profound influence on their lives. When a person moves to another place, the first thing he or she does is try to find/build a tribe.

Tribes in the New Testament are "households" or "spheres of influence"—in Greek, *oikos*. Some familiar names and examples of their tribes include:

- Zacchaeus (Luke 19:9)
- Cornelius (Acts 11:14)
- Lydia (Acts 16:15)
- Philippian Jailer (Acts 16:31-33)
- Crispus (Acts 18:8)
- Levi, the tax collector (Luke 5:27-32)

In the biblical narrative, tribes are essentially churches waiting to happen.

"Extractional Discipleship" vs. "Tribal Discipleship"

For years, many missions efforts have focused on "getting people into a local church." New Christ-followers do need a believing community but except for extreme, unhealthy cases, it may not be the best idea to rip them out of their tribes.

If Christ-followers rush to plug everyone into a church, the result is building forced, awkward groups whose members have little influence on one another. These new "Christian" relationships begin to crowd out natural, existing friendships, jeopardizing the potential for the gospel to spread among tribes.

Since people are usually already grouped—friends since grade school, neighbors, business partners, extended families, sports clubs—group-building doesn't have to be the focus of missions. Yes, it may take a long time for a tribe to come to faith as seen in the New Testament. But in the meantime, local Christian workers can encourage and pray for a new Christ-follower and the tribe he or she represents, believing that God does want that entire *oikos* to come to faith.

As your team gets into conversations with locals, listen for who their tribes are. Find out more about them. Whether your conversations turn to spiritual things or not, take time to pray for the individuals you meet and the "churches waiting to happen" that they represent.

List your initial ideas of who tribes might be in your host community. What do your local contacts say about the concept? What are the characteristics of these tribes?

With which of these tribes might you have a natural connection? When might you be able to connect with them during your trip, either during planned or unplanned activities? Who will you ask to join you (team-mate, leader, etc.)?

DO SOME CULTURAL EXEGESIS

As your team continues discovering your host city, its people, tribes, and third places, consider how you can learn even more about culture through an approach called cultural exegesis. Paul did this in Athens, as recorded in Acts 17:22-33, where he "perceived" that the Athenians were religious. He observed, commented, and told the Athenians' own story back to them in light of the gospel.

Exegesis (literally, "to draw out") is the act of studying something (text, art, language) and extracting meaning from within the work. The opposite is *eisegesis* (literally "to draw in"), in which the observer interprets the meaning through his own presuppositions.

What might cultural exegesis entail?

Values/Customs: What is important to people? How do they spend time, money, energy? Is it on family, work, friends, money, power, respect, land, independence?

Conflicts/Needs: What challenges people's values? What tension do they feel? War/peace, social issues, oppression, natural disasters, enemies, economic factors?

Outlook: Do people consider their outlook on life to be positive/negative, victor/victim, hopeful/hopeless? Is the worldview marked by socialism, capitalism, progress, class/caste systems, education, religion, tradition?

Stories: What stories are found in the culture's movies, books, TV, mythology, folk tales/songs? What are pervasive themes? Redemption, overcoming, oppression, hope, good vs. evil?

Idols: What do people worship, formally or informally? What are their (dys)functional saviors? Do people look to religion, tradition, systems/structures, technology, money, materialism, education?

Fears: Look at cultural extremes. What do people run from/defend against/avoid? War, oppression, loss of culture, loss of status, disease, exploitation, shame?

Narrative: How do people make sense of the world around them? Who is telling the stories? Social commentators, government, religion, superstition, rock stars, royalty?

Tribes: How do people organize socially? Where do they find their social identity? Subcultures, affinities, clubs, neighborhoods, stereotypes, friends, cliques?

During your trip, *use the space provided to take notes* on what you learn and compare them with your teammates. Clearly, worldviews will vary from individual to individual, but you may see some common themes emerge. As you listen, you may also discover cultural "bridges" or natural connections to the gospel.

Pray about God's work in the lives of the people you meet and in their communities and culture. Listen for how He would want you to continue learning and be involved in what He is already doing.

PART TWO: LISTEN AS YOU GO

PART TWO: LISTEN AS YOU GO

PRACTICE YOUR GEOMETRY

The Geometry of Disciple-Making: **(+ & =)** *Perpendicular & Parallel Pathways*

PERPENDICULAR PATHS

Perpendicular paths mean living in constant response to Spirit-led opportunities to proclaim the gospel and serve people.

In Scripture, followers of Jesus often had Spirit-led encounters with people they met. One such instance of this is in Acts 8:26-40, the story of Philip and the Ethiopian official.

- God directed Philip to go south on the desert road. Philip obeyed.
- God instructed Philip to go up beside a chariot. Philip obeyed.
- The Ethiopian official was seeking, reading Scripture from the prophet Isaiah.
- Philip, being in the God-appointed place, heard the Ethiopian reading the Scripture aloud, and asked him a question: "Do you understand what you are reading?"
- Philip told the official the good news about Jesus, starting with Isaiah 53:7-8.
- The official asked Philip to baptize him.
- The Spirit "carried" Philip away; he and the official had no further contact.

When you have perpendicular encounters with people that God puts in your life, it requires the Spirit's guidance, obedience, and preparation.

PARALLEL PATHS

Parallel paths mean living life in the context of the community where we are serving. Christians deliberately model for others what life in Christ could look like for someone from the local culture to follow Jesus.

The life of Jesus records multiple examples of parallel paths. One example is in Matthew 4:18-22, when Jesus called the twelve disciples:

- Jesus invited Peter and Andrew to follow Him (no explicit gospel "presentation").
- The fishermen dropped their nets and followed Jesus.
- The men spent three years being discipled by Jesus.
- Disciples ministered alongside Jesus.
- Confession and belief are a process.

This is an ongoing personal relationship with people where you live, work, and play.

Parallel discipleship requires a lifestyle of obedience and commitment to an ongoing relationship. The focus on both words and works allows for demonstration and learning-by-doing.

Read 2 Timothy 2:2.

What opportunities for perpendicular and parallel paths might you have even in your short time on the ground? List your ideas here. During and after the trip, record how you saw this "geometry" in action. Pray for those you met.

CONDUCT A DAILY DEBRIEFING

At the end of each day (or early the next morning), take a few minutes to listen to God and write down reflections on the day and how you saw Him move. Use the extra notes pages in the back to answer the debriefing questions for the duration of your trip.

Logistics: What questions or thoughts do you have from the day regarding logistics, schedule, or programming?

1.

2.

3.

Conversations: With whom did you get into a conversation? What did you talk about? How can you pray for those individuals?

1.

2.

3.

Introductions to make: *Did you meet anyone about whom you'd like your team leader or local contact to know? What opportunity might you have to introduce them to one another?*

1.

2.

3.

Tomorrow: *What do you need to know about tomorrow?*

1.

2.

3.

Go over any necessary points among your team and/or with your team and field leaders as appropriate.

PART THREE:
LISTEN AS YOU GO BACK

DEBRIEF THE TRIP AS A TEAM

Before you know it, your short-term mission trip will be drawing to a close. While we hope you've been using the Daily Debriefing guide regularly, a final end-of-trip debriefing is also helpful for individuals and teams.

Pause, listen, and reflect on the following as you close out your trip, using the space provided as desired.

Listen. *Start your time in silence, listening to God.*

Read Psalm 145 aloud. Praise God for specific ways He has revealed Himself during this time. List new things you discovered about Him. Pause to meditate on His character.

Thank God for what He has done during the trip. *Think of situations only He could have orchestrated, times He blessed you with a sense of His presence, ways He led you throughout the week, etc. As a team, share those together. After each item,* **read Psalm 107:8 aloud.**

Comment on highlights and challenges of the trip. *What went well* with logistics, programming, and other tangible items? What was the context? Who was present and involved? How did God show up? How were the situations resolved (if needed)? What follow-up would be necessary? Be sure to communicate this to the field leader(s).

How did you and the team incorporate listening into your attitude and rhythms? What did you notice about this practice? What did you "hear" for the first time from the Holy Spirit, your contacts, those you met, or your teammates?

How did your sending church participate in this experience? Make sure to thank those who were praying, helping with logistics at home, or contributing financially.

What memorable stories emerged from the week? You may wish to have someone collect those.

What did you learn during your time? Language, culture, spiritual truths, likes/dislikes, strengths and weaknesses—the sky's the limit.

How has God changed you as a result of this trip?

Would you want to return to this place at another point? *Why or why not?*

Would you want to explore future missions opportunities in this form or others? *Repeating this trip, taking a leadership role, organizing or participating in a different opportunity, looking at a mid-term or long-term missions role, meeting people from other cultures in your own hometown, pursuing a marketplace career in another location, etc. Living missionally takes many different forms.*

What would you keep the same or change for a future short-term trip?

When will you and your team share with the larger church (and/or specific groups within the church) about this experience?

What's next? *How can your team support any follow-up to be done? How can you advocate for those you met? What would God want you to share about the experience with your sending church? What might God have you talk through with your trip leader(s) or missions pastor regarding your role in His Great Commission? (See the entries "Reflect on Your Individual Experience" and "Do Try This at Home!" to go deeper.)*

LISTEN TO THE SPIRIT
AS YOU GO BACK

As mentioned previously, in Luke 10, Jesus commissioned seventy-two of His disciples to go on a short-term mission to the places He was about to minister. These were strategic places where Jesus was soon to teach, preach, and heal. He sent this group out to prepare the way, and in verses 17-20, these missionaries returned:

> The seventy-two returned with joy, saying, "Lord, even the demons are subject to us in your name!" And he said to them, "I saw Satan fall like lightning from heaven. Behold, I have given you authority to tread on serpents and scorpions, and over all the power of the enemy, and nothing shall hurt you. Nevertheless, do not rejoice in this, that the spirits are subject to you, but rejoice that your names are written in heaven."

These disciples were amazed at the work they encountered and the incredible things God did on their trip. They were filled with joy and astonishment at His power. Jesus reminded them that though they experienced incredible mission activity, they should not forget the true importance of their identity as followers of Jesus.

As you return home, remember these words. Your true worth is not in what you do or accomplish, but in your identity in Christ. What does Scripture tell you about this identity?

- Jesus described His people as salt and light (Matthew 5:13-16).
- Paul said Christians are ambassadors (2 Corinthians 5:20).
- John recorded the words of Jesus: "as the Father has sent me, even so, I am sending you" (John 20:21).

While multiple passages in Scripture highlight different aspects of our identity in Jesus, one of the key characteristics is in that last bullet point. Believers are *sent*—and not just once a year on occasional, official "mission trips" but in every moment, in every context.

The same tools that you used on your trip are at your disposal in every aspect of your life. "You will be my witnesses," Jesus said in Acts 1:8. You have a "sent" identity, regardless of whether you are a student, a working professional, a parent, a child, a full-time vocational missionary, a sibling, a job-seeker, a hobby enthusiast, a tourist, a retiree, or a million other things.

Wherever you live, work, and play, you can participate in what God is doing. Don't have a "team" outside of your short-term mission trip? Don't worry. You are never going into any of your daily contexts alone. The Holy Spirit goes with you and is with you all of the time, whether on a short-term mission trip or in your day-to-day life at home. He will provide you companions in the Body of Christ. He will still speak to you and lead you as you go into all your usual places. All you have to do is continue what you've learned through this short-term experience: listen.

REFLECT ON YOUR INDIVIDUAL EXPERIENCE

Just as we encourage your team to use the "Debrief the Trip as a Team" entry, we also believe each trip participant should take time to reflect individually on the overall trip experience and how God is using it in your life.

"Missions" isn't assigned only to the "professionals." All Christians have received the Great Commission. Hopefully, having been in a different context, you've seen some new ways that God brings that about.

How might God have you to continue your role in the Great Commission post-trip? Here are some best practices for discovering the answers (which can vary a great deal). Add your own notes about these topics in the following pages or in your own personal journal.

Listen. *Spend time in silence.*

Write down the key lessons you learned and things you experienced. *Pray over them and how God would keep using them.*

Share your experience with trusted confidants.

Study the Book of Acts and notice the different missions opportunities described: not just Paul's obvious missionary travels, but where and how else are Jesus' disciples serving Him and making Him known?

List the gifts, talents, and abilities you were able to use on this trip.

List your other gifts, talents, and abilities God could continue to use.

Consider contexts where your gifts could meet a need and that spark a natural interest in your heart. Your neighborhood? Your department at work? Your running club? Another city? A group of people from another country living in your city? Those with financial needs? Through an existing program at your church? Those with emotional needs? God has already placed you among people who need Him. While the setting may change, the call remains constant.

Speak with your church leadership as appropriate to explore existing opportunities, both formal and informal.

REPORT BACK TO YOUR SENDING CHURCH

Initially, we mentioned that some of the key individuals involved in your trip didn't come on your trip at all. They were supporting from home through prayers, encouragement, and even financial support. Now that you're back from your short-term mission trip, how can you let them know what their support meant to you?

Paul and Barnabas are a biblical example of this in Acts 14. Read through chapters 14 and 15, and then zero in on 14:26-27.

What were the circumstances before and after their return to Antioch?

Why was Antioch special to them?

PART THREE: LISTEN AS YOU GO BACK

What did they do while among the Antioch church?

Like Paul and Barnabas in this scenario, mission trip teams typically give some kind of report to the whole church upon their return. But what you may envision—perhaps a worship center, PowerPoint, emotional video presentation format—isn't your only option. Yes, you want to let the larger church know what their support has meant and how God has used their willingness to partner with you in this initiative. But your team can also be creative in how you choose to share what has taken place.

Start with listening. Listen to the Lord individually and as a group to see what He might want you to share about your experiences. Are there stories that stand out? A particular message? A specific passage or concept from Scripture?

Also, what are the questions you received from church members prior to going? What questions have people asked along the way in response to any prayer updates, social media posts, etc.? What are they not asking?

What is the best forum to share what God has done? Has your pastor planned for the team to take up a great part of a typical service? Would an additional meeting for interested individuals be more appropriate? Are there Bible study groups, volunteers, and specific leadership who need to know how the trip went and what God is doing in the community you visited? Does the entire team need to be in front of every different type of audience?

As you explore these outlets, pray about what will be the most meaningful way to talk about God's work in the community, allow for questions and dialogue, and also inspire others to dream about their role in missions.

What media will be most effective for your audiences? Creativity is encouraged. Is a recap on social media the way to go? Did your team produce a video? Are simple photos enough? Is it helpful to share how donated resources were used? Do you have an exceptional storyteller in your group who could best convey the most important aspects of the trip? Do you want to list the answers to prayers from your sending church? Is there a song that encapsulates the spirit of your time serving together? Perhaps it is a combination of several elements.

What will you do with continued interest from people within the church? If someone is inspired to get involved in a different way, what suggestions could your team and church leadership give for next steps? How could you encourage interested individuals to explore their part in the Great Commission? Would it be appropriate or beneficial for others from your church to be put in touch with those who were part of the community you served? While your church leadership may have suggestions ready, your team may also have some creative ideas for continuing to involve others in God's work in the place you were.

DO TRY THIS AT HOME!

You've returned from your short-term mission trip and are back into the groove of daily life at home. But is that it? Do all the experiences and stories simply fade into memory?

They don't have to, and God certainly hasn't stopped working just because an event seems to be over. He continues His kind, loving, patient labor in the lives of all involved.

While a mission trip is unique, intense, and even life-changing, the call to "go" isn't reserved exclusively for unfamiliar places. Actually, the majority of our "going" must take place on a daily basis.

What if mission trip participants applied what they learned in their day-to-day contexts? What might that look like? What impact might it have for the Kingdom?

Here are a few examples of concepts could translate into your world:

Listening. If Christ-followers stop listening just because the context is familiar, everyone is in big trouble! The time and stillness you and your team have dedicated to listening to the Holy Spirit is a practice easily incorporated in any setting. We should also continue to listen to our co-laborers in Christ right where we are, as well as the people we meet in our own cities.

Prayer. Just as a missions team prays individually and together, prayer is a discipline everyone can embrace on a regular basis. It is a lifeline to God and a special way for Him to reveal what He is up to—and how to be part of it.

Cultural Research. The world has become smaller as international mobility has become more feasible. "Every tribe and language and people and nation" (Revelation 5:9) is likely to be found closer than you think! You may already know neighbors, co-workers, and friends from different cultural backgrounds. Have you considered other nationalities represented in your hometown?

If you went on an international mission trip, now you know what it's like to be in a different country. Could God use your experience as a "foreigner" to help you minister to those who find themselves outside their own countries?

Could you somehow serve those who have recently moved to your city from another country? Do you simply want to get to know them? Could you again embrace the attitude of being a learner and make an effort to learn about the people and cultures represented in your city?

Mapping, Prayerwalking, and Third Places. Sure, you may think you know your neighborhood and typical routes like the back of your hand, but what if you apply the mapping concepts to see your city with new eyes? What if you noticed those whom you pass on a daily basis and considered that God might be crossing your paths for a reason? What if you walked or drove prayerfully on your way to work or to run errands? What if you took notice of where people were gathering and creating community? What if you joined the existing "tribes" where your interests naturally lie, bringing the presence of Christ with you? Your intentionality could just pave the way for something big in your own hometown.

Storytelling. Now that you've thought about your walk with Christ as a series of testimonies, your storytelling certainly isn't limited to a different place. Actually, God will continue to invite Himself into conversations and give you opportunities to tell stories about Him to others. You just have to listen and be prepared to join Him.

"Gospel Conversations." Likewise, sharing the gospel verbally doesn't stop. In fact, when we internalize the good news and are experiencing it regularly, it becomes a natural part of our conversations wherever we are. Again, we'll want to listen and be sensitive to those around us and what God is doing, but "sharing the gospel" doesn't have to be a foreign concept even at home.

The Geometry of Disciple-Making. At home, God will still present you with the opportunity to disciple others, both in parallel and perpendicular ways. Who are those people for you? Are they your children? Are they teenagers you teach? Are they peers? Pray about what disciple-making looks like for you in your home context.

You get the idea: there actually isn't that big a difference between approaching a mission trip and a truly missional lifestyle. Physical surroundings, cultures, activities, and languages may change, but the same prayerful outlook is necessary, the same humble, listening attitude is required. Contexts look different, but God brings His Kingdom to earth in multiple ways in all of them.

Spend some time writing about ways He might have you apply the things you've learned in your settings. We pray you'll stay just as attentive, listening always for His invitation to join Him in His work at home and around the world.

APPENDICES

APPENDIX 1: A WORLDVIEW CASE STUDY FROM SCRIPTURE

To help you better grasp the idea of what worldview is and how it influences ministry, look at part of Paul's time in Athens, as told in Acts 17:12-32.

Did Paul discern the worldview of many of the Athenians? If so, how?

What might have been cultural barriers to presenting the gospel in this setting?

What cultural "bridges" to the gospel did Paul use?

In this chapter of Acts, Paul is an observer and a listener among the Athenians. He notices the idolatry present in the city and the absence of any knowledge of the Lord.

Physically, Paul puts himself on-site and in a position to interact with the people of Athens in the synagogue and in the marketplace. He listens and takes in what he is learning and seeing from Jewish people, God-fearing Greek people, and even Epicurean and Stoic philosophers. The philosophers then invited him into a meeting in which they asked about what he was preaching.

Paul astutely meets them where they are as intellectuals and philosophers. He does not seem to appeal to the Scriptures, which they do not know as he does, but to evidence that their culture would value and in references that they themselves understand: speaking about nature, quoting their poets, and introducing the truth of Jesus' resurrection.

The outcome of this bold foray into the local worldview and setting was that people like Dionysius and Damaris believed Paul's message, and others asked Paul to return for further discussion.

While you may not have the exact same experience, pray about what God would have you listen for and observe about the local worldview where you are going. Ask Him to make evident to you the cultural connections to the gospel, the perspectives of those you encounter, and when and where He might have you speak about Him to others.

APPENDIX 2: PACK YOUR BAGS

THE ESSENTIALS—WHAT NOT TO FORGET

This is meant to be a general guide. Ask your team leader about the specifics of packing for your trip.

Carry-on Bag:
- ☐ Airplane tickets/itinerary.
- ☐ Immunization records and proof of recent health screenings, if required.
- ☐ Passport/visa. DO NOT pack your passport in your checked luggage.
- ☐ Cash and credit/debit cards: keep in a safe place. (Access your accounts online and set up a travel notification for each card. Or, you can call the customer service number on each card and ask them to note the dates and countries of your travel on your account.)
- ☐ Two extra passport photos (ask team leader if this is needed).
- ☐ A good book.
- ☐ Bible, journal, and pen.
- ☐ Extra glasses, especially if you wear contacts.
- ☐ All prescription medications in their original containers, with a copy of the prescriptions.
- ☐ Travel size toiletry items: shampoo, soap, cleansers, toothbrush/paste/floss, comb/brush, hand sanitizer, tissue, small pack of hand wipes, deodorant (no tweezers, razors, or pocket knives!).
- ☐ Remember the rule of liquids/gels/creams when flying: 3-1-1. No liquid, gel, or cream can exceed three ounces (by listed volume). All items must be packed in a 1-quart-sized, clear, plastic, zip-top bag, with a limit of one bag per passenger in carry-ons. Greater

quantities of liquids or gels must be placed in checked luggage or left behind.

- ☐ One extra set of clothes: your luggage may not arrive when you do. You will want an extra set of clean clothes to wear while you are waiting for your luggage to catch up to you.
- ☐ Emergency contact information.
- ☐ Photocopy of your passport.

Checked Luggage:

- ☐ Clothing (Remember: climate, culture, and your project assignment. See "Pack Smart; Pack Light.")
  - ☐ Men: Ask if you need button-up shirts/polos, khakis, tie, etc. If you are teaching or in a business setting, you will need to dress appropriately.
  - ☐ Women: Ask about sleeve length, shirt length, and skirt length. Are skirts or pants more appropriate? Are shorts allowed? Do you need a scarf/head covering?
  - ☐ Underwear: Avoid nylon, which doesn't dry well and can lead to fungal infections in hot climates.
- ☐ Comfortable shoes: If appropriate, you may want to choose sports/ hiking shoes or sandals.
- ☐ Hat, if necessary, for protection from the sun.
- ☐ Camera (if not using your phone's camera) and charger/extra batteries. (If valuable, put it in your carry-on.)
- ☐ Toiletries: see list above. Always pack liquids in Ziplocs!
- ☐ First-aid items: band-aids, hand sanitizer, antibiotic cream, Pep-to-bismol, Imodium, ibuprofen, sunscreen/lip balm with sunscreen.
- ☐ Toilet tissue: never a bad idea to have some on hand!
- ☐ Insect repellent.
- ☐ Feminine products: these are not available in many countries.
- ☐ Quick-dry towels/washcloths, if your team leader says linens are not provided.
- ☐ Ministry-related materials: ask your team leader what might be necessary.
- ☐ A few extra Ziploc bags and plastic grocery bags.
- ☐ Gifts for your field leader(s)/hosts: ask if there are things they would like from the U.S.
- ☐ Pictures of your family and friends, in case those are helpful in conversations as you meet people. Make sure people in your pictures are dressed appropriately.
- ☐ Razors (with extra blades, if not disposable).
- ☐ Rain jacket/umbrella/poncho, depending on assignment.

APPENDIX 3: INTERNATIONAL TRIP PRE-TRAVEL CHECKLIST

These tips are given primarily for a U.S.-based audience. If your church is based in another country, research the local equivalents in government agencies, legal requirements, health precautions, etc.

EMERGENCY
- ☐ Police/Ambulance/Fire and/or local 911 equivalent
- ☐ Embassy address and phone number for all countries to be visited Names, addresses, and phone numbers of hospitals that treat/ are safe for foreigners (start with The U.S. Department of State)
- ☐ Cell phone numbers for your hosts or travel company
- ☐ Personal emergency contact at home

LEGAL
- ☐ Leave a copy of your passport, visa, itinerary, important phone numbers, and health-related documents with the contact person of your choice at home.
- ☐ Designate a Power-of-Attorney so a trusted contact at home can make important decisions on your behalf, should you not be able to.
- ☐ Make sure you have a will in place.
- ☐ Authorize someone to take care of your finances if your return is delayed.

FINANCES
- ☐ Let banks and credit card companies know of your travel plans, including dates and places.
- ☐ Find the best way to exchange money for where you are going and at what point to do it.

- ☐ Consider paying pending bills before you leave the country, as payment online may not be available or secure overseas. You could also speak with a trusted friend or family member about how he or she could help you with any pending payments during your trip.

COMMUNICATION

- ☐ Verify conditions of cell phone use where you are going, and/or purchase a global plan.

HEALTH

- ☐ Check with the CDC or local Health Department for suggested/ required immunizations and health screenings.
- ☐ Let your doctor know that you are traveling internationally.
- ☐ Request a broad-based antibiotic that treats bacterial or parasitic illness.
- ☐ Buy international travel insurance that includes emergency medical evacuation coverage.

RESOURCES

- ☐ Mobile Passport app: allows U.S. citizens and Canadian visitors to skip long immigration lines during entry into many major U.S. airports.
- ☐ The U.S. Department of State's Smart Traveler Enrollment Program: access to current official country information, travel alerts, travel warnings, maps, U.S. embassy locations, etc.
- ☐ Online translation applications, if necessary (Google Translate may do the trick in a bind).
- ☐ U.S. Department of State website

APPENDIX 4: SAMPLE COMMISSIONING LITURGY

Introduction: Today, we have the joy of sending out *[number of individuals]* to live and proclaim the gospel among the nations. Let me introduce *[names]*. *[Name]* is our lead international missions pastor over all campuses and *[Name]* serves as the missions pastor here at *[church name]*. Pastors, lead us in this special time of commissioning.

Pastor: With us this morning are *[participants]*.

[Participants come and stand in front of the stage. Leaders give introductions and speak affirmation over those being sent.]

Pastor: Commissioning these individuals means, quite simply, that we as a church are sending them. To truly be sent, one must have a home. So when we say we're sending you, we're also making a commitment; you have a home here.

It's been a long journey of preparation to be standing here today. And now before the Lord, and before this church, we invite you to make the following commitments:

To participants: Since the gospel is the world's only hope, do you commit to abide in Christ, to live and proclaim Him alongside other Christians, to remember His church that sent you, and to maintain your hope in Him when trials inevitably come? If so, say, "We do."

Participants: We do.

[Leaders turn to the church]

Pastor: If you're a member of this church, or someone who is here out of a commitment to love and support these individuals, please stand with me.

Friends, the pastors of this church commend these men and women to you as godly leaders, whose lives and motives have been examined, and whom we believe the Lord has called to go to the ends of the earth for the sake of the gospel.

To Church: Do you commit to supporting them with prayer, friendship, and financial resources, not forgetting that they are extensions of our church family? If so, say, "We do."

Church: We do.

Pastor: We want to invite family members, elders, and those that have committed to care for these individuals to come forward and lay hands on them now.

[Staff and leaders lead in prayer over commissioning participants.][10]

ENDNOTES

[1] "Worldview Definitions," *Your Dictionary*: www.yourdictionary.com/worldview.

[2] Adapted from Lloyd E. Kwast, "Understanding Culture" in *Perspectives on the World Christian Movement: A Reader*, eds. Ralph D. Winter and Steven C. Hawthorne (Pasadena, CA: William Carey Library, 2013).

[3] Categories and descriptions adapted from Kevin Lynch, *The Image of the City* (Cambridge, MA: The MIT Press, 1960).

[4] Adapted from Jill D. Burruss and Lisa Kaenzig, "Introversion: The Often Forgotten Factor Impacting the Gifted," *Virginia Association for the Gifted Newsletter* 21 no.1 (Fall 1999).

[5] Adapted from Sojourn Community Church Midtown's Short-Term Trips.

[6] "Prayer Walking: Praying On-Site With Insight," by Steve Hawthorne and Graham Kendrick.

[7] Adapted from writings by Thom Wolf.

[8] Ray Oldenburg, *The Great Good Place* (New York: Marlowe and Company, 1989).

[9] Michael Frost, *Exiles: Living Missionally in a Post-Christian Culture* (Grand Rapids: Baker Books, 2006) 56-59.

[10] Reproduced with permission from the Sojourn Collective in Louisville, KY.

NOTES

NOTES